ANIMAL WAYS

ANIMALS AT HOME

Jane Burton

Newington Press

First published in the United States in 1991 by
Newington Press
2 Old New Milford Road, Brookfield, CT 06804
Text copyright © Jane Burton 1991
Photographs copyright © Jane Burton and
Kim Taylor 1991

First published in Great Britain in 1991 by
Belitha Press Limited

Cataloging-in-Publication Data
Burton, Jane
Animals at home / Jane Burton;
photographs Jane Burton and Kim Taylor.
Brookfield, CT, Newington Press, 1991.
24 p.; ill.;
Includes glossary and index.
ISBN 1-878137-12-3
1. Animals—Habitations.   2. Animal societies.
3. Animals—Infancy.   4. Animals—Habits
and behavior.   I. Title.   II. Jane Burton, photographer.   III. Kim Taylor, photographer.

Contents

Where do animals live?

There is life almost everywhere on earth. Almost every bit of the earth provides a **habitat** where certain kinds of animals make their home.

Deserts are hot and dry. Only animals suited to these conditions can live there. While other animals would die of heat or thirst, camels are suited to the desert. Camels can get quite hot during the day without it doing them harm. Camels can go for days without drinking water. When

camels do find water they drink a huge amount at one time. But they know to stop before they harm themselves by drinking too much. When there is plenty of food they put on fat. This is stored in their humps to be used when food is scarce.

Gerbils are desert animals. They are so small that if they came out in the day the hot sand would scorch them. They spend the day underground to keep cool and come out only at night. Gerbils get all the **moisture** they need from the seeds they eat.

Deserts are poor habitats. There is not much to eat, so only a few animals live there. Some habitats are so rich they teem with wildlife. Salt lake water is too foul and salty to drink, but a few sorts of tiny animals and plants thrive there in countless millions.

From a distance this salt lake seems to have a pink shore. In fact, the shore is covered with thousands of pink flamingos. Their beaks strain tiny plants out of shallow water. Sometimes half a million flamingos wade and feed together around the edge of this lake.

Flocks of fish-eating birds feed on the schools of fish living in salt lakes. The biggest fish-eaters are white pelicans. They swim in a horseshoe formation, driving the fish into a tight bunch in front of them. Then the pelicans plunge their heads underwater and catch the fish in their throat pouches. When they lift their heads, the water drains from their beaks and they swallow the fish they have caught.

Sometimes cormorants hunt with the pelicans. They fish by diving and swimming underwater. After the birds have eaten their fill they come ashore to **preen.**

How do they live?

The earth's weather is rarely mild all the time. Most places are either hot or cold. Some are very hot in summer and very cold in winter. Animals that live in such places have found ways to survive these extreme conditions.

Striped pixie toads live in dry places. But toads need water to lay their eggs in, so when it rains the pixies gather in puddles to **spawn.** Soon, however, the sun dries the puddles up. The pixies' eggs must develop quickly and hatch in only two or three days. The pixie tadpoles start feeding almost right away. They grow so fast that they double their weight in the first day, then double it again the day after.

As their puddle starts to dry up, the tadpoles band together and wriggle so that their tails stir up the mud. This deepens the water in the puddle and stops it from drying up so fast. And it gives the tadpoles just enough time to grow legs and begin to breathe air before the water is all gone. Then the toadlets hop out of the mud and search for a large stone they can hide under to stay damp.

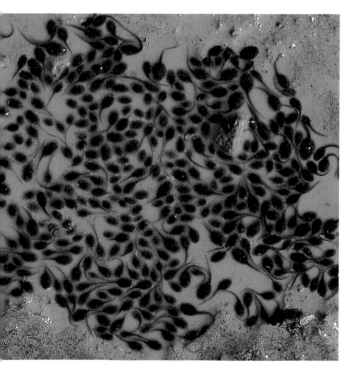 

Different animals that live in the same way are often a similar shape, because that shape best suits their way of life. Animals that swim have smooth **streamlined** bodies that cut through water with as little effort as possible.

Gray mullet zip along like torpedoes by beating their tails from side to side. Hawksbill turtles propel themselves through the water with their front flippers and steer with their rudderlike hind feet. Penguins seem to fly through the water the way other birds fly through the air. They use their wings as flippers, and their tubby bodies are smooth and boat-shaped.

▲ Bottle-nosed dolphins have a layer of fat, or blubber, under the skin that makes them smooth and streamlined. Dolphins can swim very fast. They beat their tails up and down rather than from side to side like fish. They steer and balance with their fins.

Many water-living animals are not streamlined at all. Edible crabs are built more like tanks than speedboats. ▲ They are at home among the rocks at the bottom of the sea. They can swim by running sideways through the water, but usually they scuttle over the rocks. They are the wrong shape to swim fast.

Monkeys and squirrels are at home in trees. They have special bodies and special skills to suit them to an active life among the branches.

◀ This spot-nosed monkey has forward-looking eyes that are good at judging distances for accurate leaps and landings. A monkey scampers along a branch with its long tail held out behind. If it leaps one way its tail swings the other way as a **counterbalance.**

Bushbabies have handlike paws that grasp firmly the ▲ instant they touch a branch or twig. If they fell they could be badly hurt.

Some animals are at home in only one habitat. Others are at home almost anywhere. Cats can climb trees but they are not true tree-dwellers. They have sharp, curved claws for clinging, and they can climb upward easily. The trouble comes when they need to get down again. Unlike squirrels, they cannot come down headfirst. They have to go down backward, then turn and jump the last little bit. Cats are really more at home on the ground, but they can **adapt** and make themselves at home in many places.

Brown rats are very adaptable. They can run, jump, climb, and swim. They are not fussy feeders at all. They eat the food that people throw away, so they are at home in towns and cities. In the country they eat grain and other crops. On the seashore they gnaw dead crabs. On islands they eat seabirds' eggs. Rats can live in houses and barns, down sewers or in burrows, in trees or among rocks, where there are people or where there are none. Rats can make themselves at home just about anywhere.

How do they live together?

Many different animals share the same habitat. Some are colored to match their surroundings. This hides them from **predators** that might eat them and from their own **prey.**

Many animals that live among plants have stripes as **camouflage.** The stripes imitate patterns of light and shade to hide the animal. Discus are timid fish that live in weedy water. They can make their stripes darken or fade. A strong stripe down the face hides the eye, making the fish even harder to spot.

◀ Green mantis and bush-cricket **nymphs** make good snacks for insect-eating birds. Both are well camouflaged among the green leaves. This mantis has seen a speckled bush-cricket and is ready to snap it up. The bush-cricket might leap away in time.

This yellow crab spider is an exact match for the butter- ▼ cup in which she lurks. An unsuspecting honeybee failed to see her and got caught. On different colored flowers crab spiders may be white or cream. On leaves they are green.

Seashore animals can live underwater when the tide is in, and out of water when the tide is out. Each kind has its own special place on the shore.

◀ Sandhoppers live on the tide line among rotting seaweed. When the tide is out they move down the beach. As the tide comes in they scramble back ahead of the waves.

Beadlet anemones and common starfish live lower down the shore, under rocks and seaweed. This anemone has ▼ contracted to protect its delicate **tentacles.** When the sea flows back it will open up again.

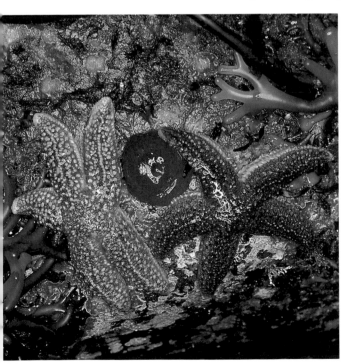

Many animals of the same sort can live together in the same habitat if they all eat something different. Three similar kinds of birds live together in waterlily swamps.

▲ Lilytrotters have very long toes that spread their weight so that they can walk on the floating lily pads without sinking. Purple gallinules have long toes too, but they are ▶ so heavy that they have to run across the lily pads. If they stand still, they will fall through. Black crakes are so light that the floating leaves hardly stir beneath their weight.

All three sorts of bird peck busily as they go, feeding on insects and water snails, tiny fish, tadpoles, seeds, and bits of waterweed. They are not in **competition** with each other, however. Since their beaks vary in size they all eat food of a different size.

The crakes can only manage tiny items such as baby ▼ snails. The gallinules can eat fairly large water snails, so they don't bother with the little ones. The midsized lilytrotters eat things that are halfway between. No one sort of bird competes with another sort for the available food.

Animals share their living space with other sorts of animals that do not compete with them. But they protect their food and nesting sites from their own kind.

◀ This male starling flutters and sings so hard that his beak and wings are a blur. Other starlings hear and see him and know that his nest is nearby.

When another red fox comes this way it will smell the scent left by this fox and know that it lives here.

A fringed filefish signals by lowering a flap under its chin. ▼ This makes it look bigger and warns other filefish that this part of the reef is *this* filefish's home.

Index / Glossary